SCHIRMER'S LIBRARY
OF MUSICAL CLASSICS

Vol. 2092

JACQUES-FÉRÉOL MAZAS

Seventy-Five Melodious and Progressive Studies
Complete
Books 1-3, Op. 36

Violin

Edited by Friedrich Hermann

ISBN 978-1-4234-9091-3

G. SCHIRMER, Inc.

DISTRIBUTED BY

HAL•LEONARD®
CORPORATION
7777 W. BLUEMOUND RD. P.O. BOX 13819 MILWAUKEE, WI 53213

www.schirmer.com
www.halleonard.com

CONTENTS

Eighteen Artists' Studies, Op. 36, Book III

Thirty Special Studies
Op. 36, Book I

Exercise on the *Crescendo* and *Decrescendo*

Jacques-Féréol Mazas
(1782–1849)

The Sweeping Stroke

The Firm Stroke

Vigorous stroke from middle to point,
the bow not quitting the string.

The Sweeping Stroke

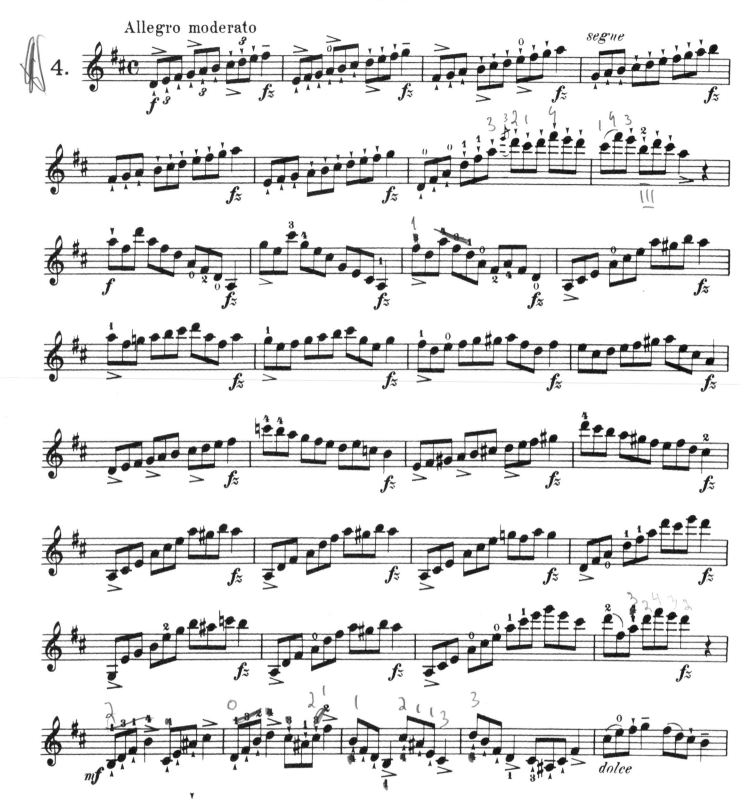

Detached Tones *(sustained)*

Allegro non troppo   Middle of bow

Detached Tones
Vigorously from middle to point

Allegro non troppo

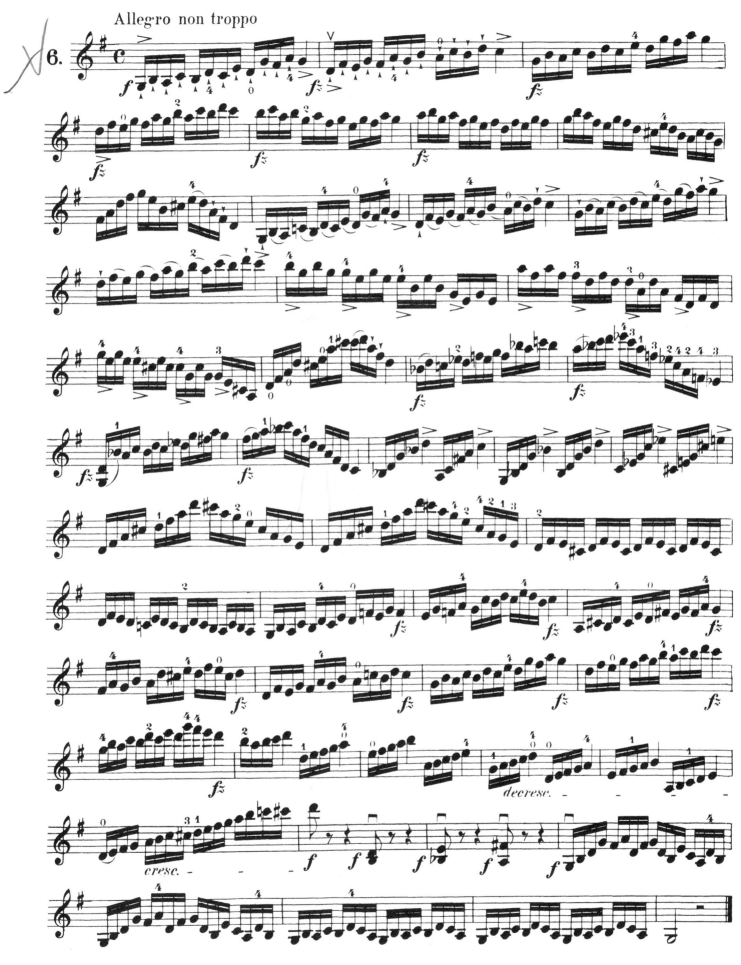

Andante

7.

Division of the Bow in the *Cantilena*

March
Allegro moderato

9.

con espressione

cresc. -

f

Vigorously, with the point of the bow

Allegro non troppo

10.

f

fz

fz

fz

Cross the strings without lifting the bow

(From middle to point)

Allegro non troppo

11.

The first note with vigorous *martellato*

Preparatory Exercise for the Trill

The Trill

Allegro moderato

15.

Various Bowings

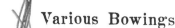

17.

18.

Finger-exercise

Flexibility of the Wrist
At the point with short bows

The same Exercise in Triplets

Short staccato strokes, and octaves

The Mordent

Allegretto grazioso

24.

dolce

Fine

dal Segno senza replica, sino al **Fine**

At the nut of the bow, lifting the bow for each note

Polonaise
Allegro moderato

26.

Singing tones, and Double-stops

Ease and lightness of bowing

Allegretto

28.

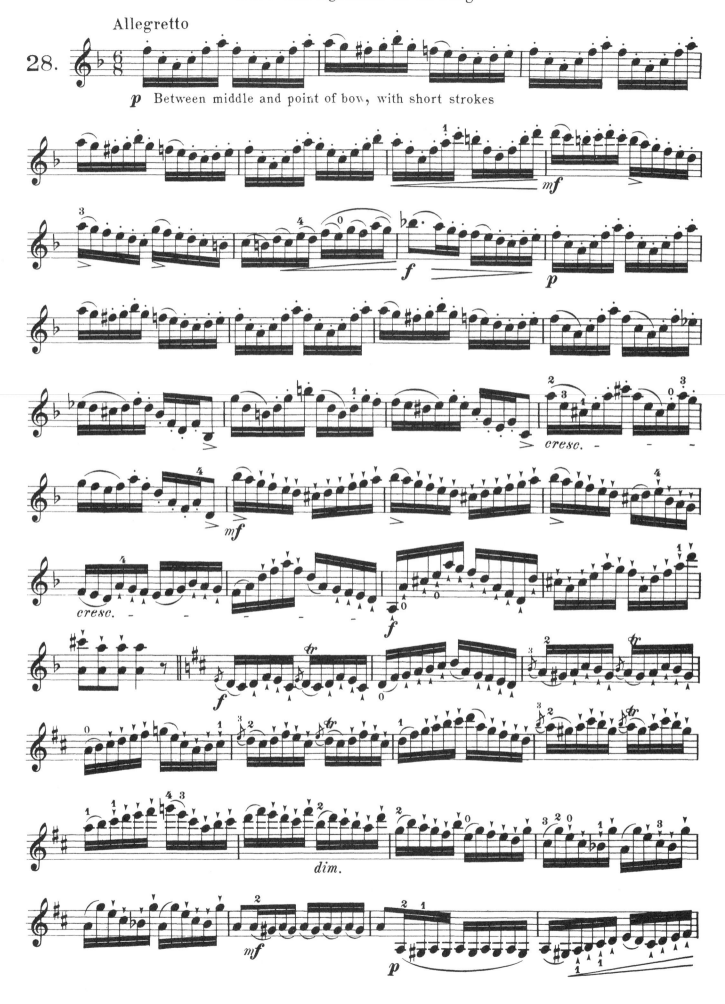

p Between middle and point of bow, with short strokes

f (the same position)

42

44

Pizzicato with the left hand

Twenty-Seven Brilliant Studies
Op. 36, Book II

Mélodie

Jacques-Féréol Mazas
(1782–1849)

The Legato

32. Allegro moderato

Bowing-exercise

33.

The Staccato

Melody on the G-string

35. Andante sostenuto

The Martellato
Bowing-exercise

Firm stroke from middle to point
Allegro moderato assai

36.

The Arpeggio
Bowing-exercise

Allegro moderato

37.

The Portamento

Andante sostenuto

38.

Bowing-exercise on two strings, for flexibility of the wrist

Embellishments of the Melody

Andante cantabile

40.

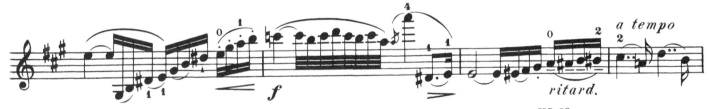

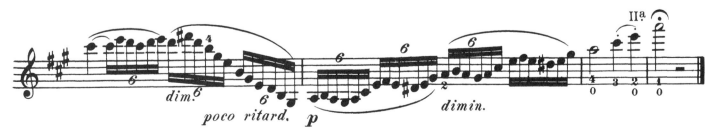

The Accented Appoggiatura

Bowing-exercise

At the point, with short bow
Allegro

42.

p leggiero

Bowing-exercise

Various Bowings

68

Springing Bow

69

Lifting the Bow

Staccato

Grazioso

Dal segno al Fine

Bowing-exercise

Bowing-exercise

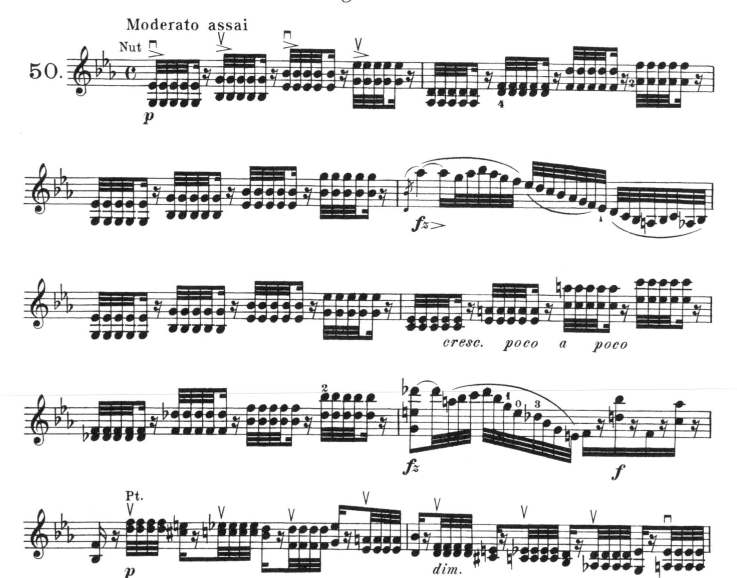

Lifting the Bow

Bowing-exercise

Well marked at the point of the bow
Allegro non troppo

Bowing-exercise

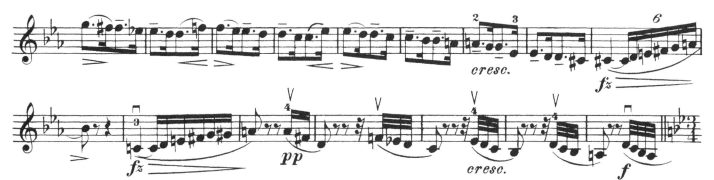

Finger-exercise

Allegro vivace

54.

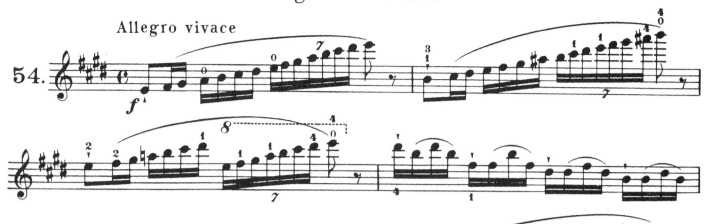

D.C.

Trill-exercise

Exercise on the Mordent

Pizzicato with the left hand (indicated by +) and Harmonics

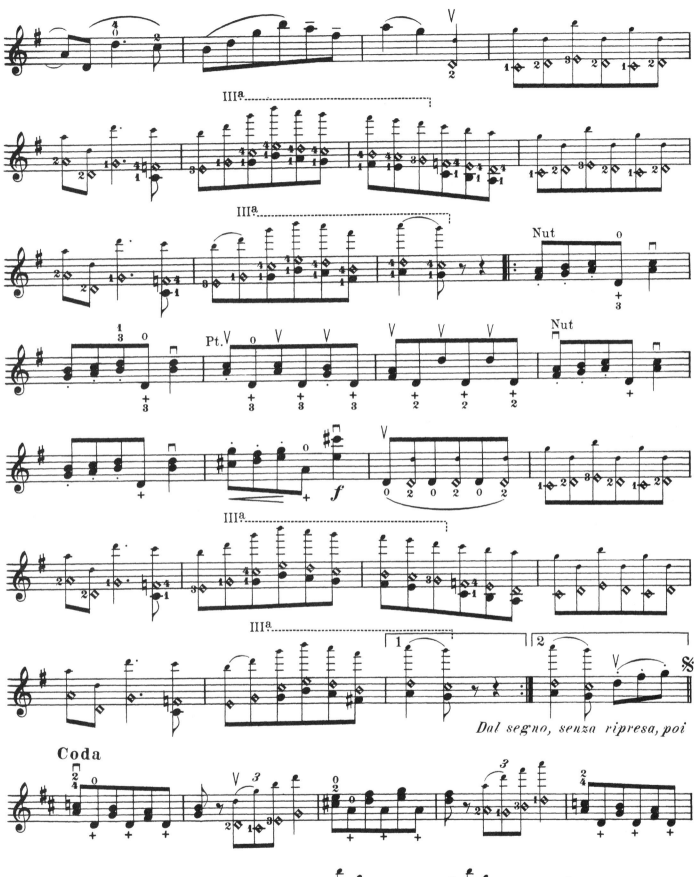

Dal segno, senza ripresa, poi

Coda

Eighteen Artist's Studies
Op. 36, Book III

Jacques-Féréol Mazas
(1782–1849)

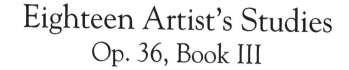

Andante

59.

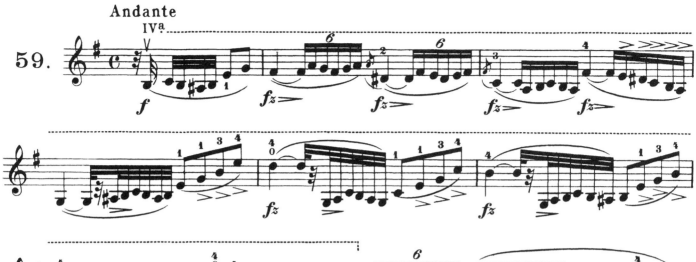

The chords with down-bow, generally from the nut

Allegro moderato

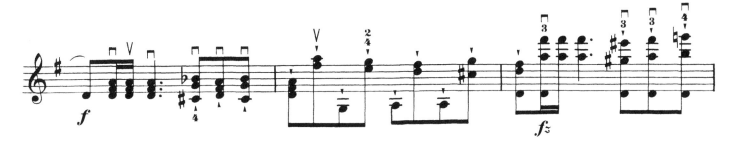

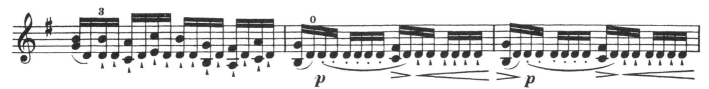

Introduction
Andante

62.

In this exercise all chords are to be taken with down-bow, and from the nut.

Allegro marziale

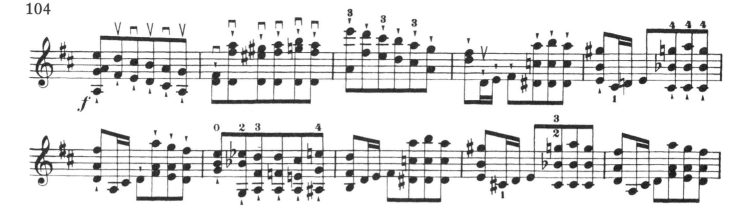

Introduction
Andante

63.

Allegro moderato

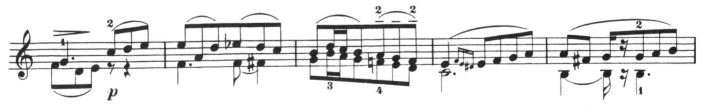

Tempo I *(Allegro moderato)*

Andante con moto

64.

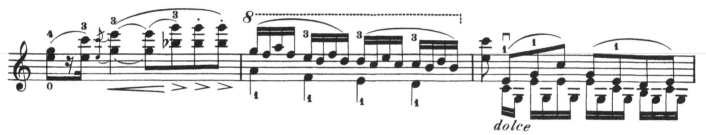

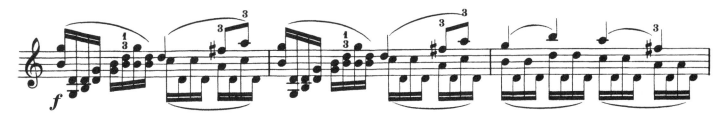

Allegro

Tarentella
Allegro vivace

65.

Più animato

non tanto mosso

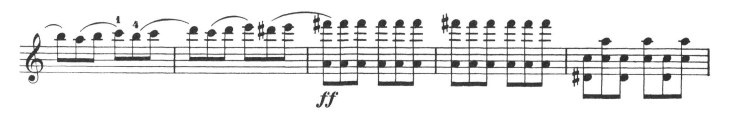

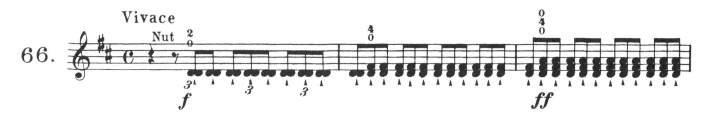

Allegro militare

Tremolo with bow on string *(not springing)*

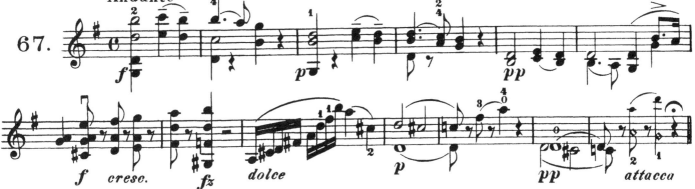

Exercise on the Tremolo legato

(Rapidly repeated finger-stroke in *legato* playing)

The half-note indicates the finger which executes the trill. Practise slowly at first, and observe throughout the value of the notes as written out in the first four measures of the *Andante*.

Tremolo with springing bow

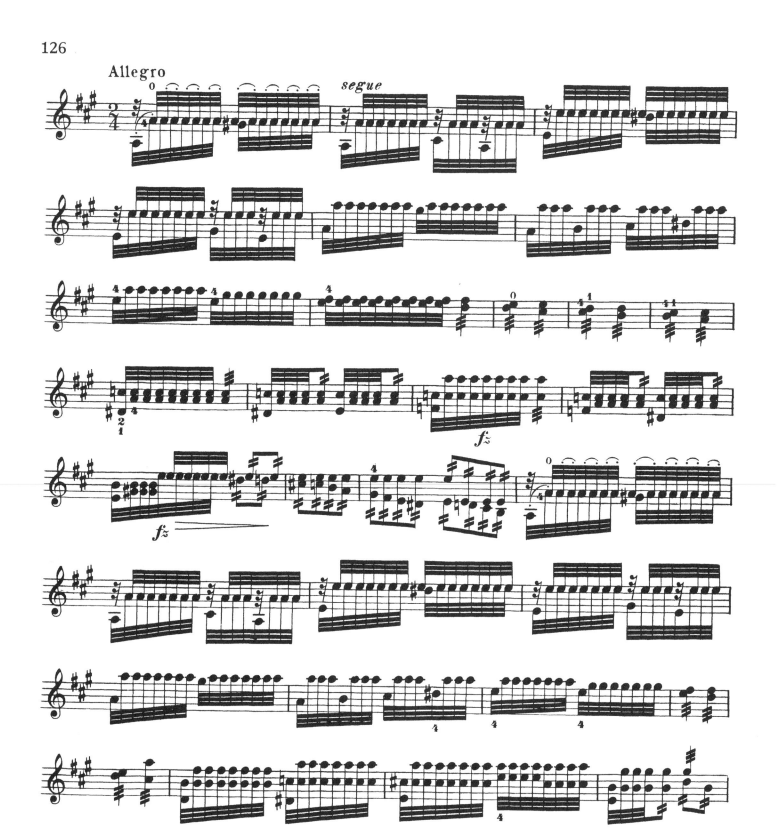

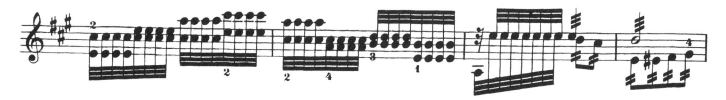

Arpeggio exercise

On three strings

Practise, at first, with simple detached bowing, middle of bow, very short, and without quitting the string, and marking the bass notes. In the second style, the springing bow sounds two tones both with down-bow and with up-bow.

70.

The preceding exercise, with three notes instead of two

Legato Arpeggios

Arpeggios of three notes, on the four strings

Arpeggios of four notes on the four strings

Play this study with a firm bow, without quitting the string, and accent each first note in the groups of four.

Maestoso sostenuto

75.

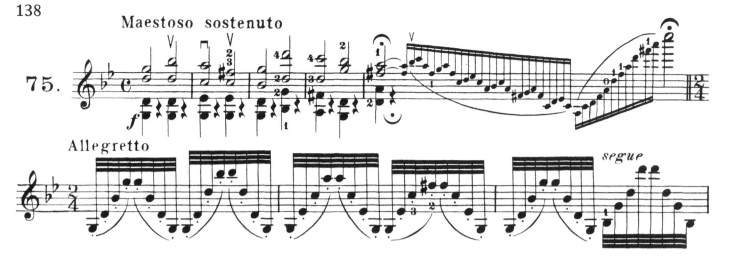

Allegretto

segue

pp *segue*

Maestoso

Tempo I

Sostenuto

Tempo I